Dragonsblood

A Story by Eugene Schwartz

Illustrated by Kris Carlson

I0810905

Cover art: Kris Carlson
Cover design: Claude Julien and John Wihl

ISBN 978-0-945803-97-3

Printed by Sierra Copy & Printing, Sacramento, CA

Book orders may be made through Rudolf Steiner College Bookstore.
Tel: 916-961-8729, Fax: 916-961-3032
Online orders: www.steinercollege.edu
E-mail: bookstore@steinercollege.edu

Rudolf Steiner College Press
9200 Fair Oaks Blvd.
Fair Oaks, CA 95628, U.S.A.

To my dear daughter Zoë

Once upon a time, there was a village ruled by a Dragon.

Every evening, the Dragon would slink out of his lair in the dark forest and appear at the village gate, hungrily demanding his due. And every evening, a chosen villager, filled with fear and trembling, would offer up to the Dragon a prize lamb, or calf, or goat.

So it went for many years. Villagers who had been children on that fateful night when the Dragon first appeared had grown up and had children of their own. Those children had grown up and had children of their own. The Dragon alone seemed never to age. He only grew ever more hungry.

One year there was a drought, which parched the grass and crops that the villagers' animals needed for their food. The cows grew lean, the sheep scrawny, and many goats and pigs died. There came a day when the villagers could no longer offer the Dragon any food that he deemed acceptable.

On the evening of that day, the Dragon slinked out of his lair in the dark forest and appeared at the village gate, hungrily demanding his due. A group of villagers, their hats in their hands, told him of the drought, and the deaths of their animals.

The Dragon listened, and then he laughed.

"You still have your children," he said, "Every evening I will accept one of them!"

"Never!" cried the villagers.

The Dragon pursed his scaly lips and blew a stream of flame at a wooden hut near the village gate. In a moment it had burned to the ground.

"Give me a child every night," said the Dragon, "Or your village, and all those who live in it, will be consumed in flames!"

He laughed again, and disappeared into the forest.

Unbeknownst to their parents, many of the village children were hidden behind trees and bushes while the Dragon made his threat. Even as their parents lived numbly from day to day, fearing the monster but unable to act against him, the older children had been planning his overthrow. Within the depths of a cave outside the village walls they had quietly built a smithy, and had learned from an aged blacksmith the secret of fashioning armor, forging swords and hammering shields.

That night, they polished their weapons and chose the twelve eldest and strongest amongst them to challenge the Dragon. Led by Michael, a shepherd's son, and Mary, a farmer's daughter, the twelve champions pledged to support one another forever.

To his parents' dismay, Michael offered himself as the first sacrifice. Yet the villagers despaired even more when he appeared that evening clothed in armor, with a gleaming sword in his right hand and a shield in his left, and announced that he would battle the Dragon to the death.

Hardly had he spoken when the Dragon slithered up to the village gate. When Michael challenged him, the Dragon laughed and spat flame through his teeth, but the boy stood his ground. When the Dragon pulled back his head, as though to strike, Michael advanced and struck a blow against the monster's scaly neck. The Dragon writhed in pain and Michael raised his sword again and struck a blow so hard that the Dragon's head fell to the ground.

Laughter bubbled from the black blood that coursed out of the Dragon's head, and the cry,

"I will return!"

In a moment, the Dragon's neck sprouted two new heads, each more fierce than the first, each laughing and spewing flame.

As Michael renewed his battle, Mary appeared with sword and shield and joined her friend. They succeeded in severing the two new heads. Laughter bubbled from the black blood that coursed out of the two heads, and the cry,

"I will return!"

Three heads now sprouted from the scaly neck, and a third child joined Michael and Mary in their combat.

For hours the battle raged. Every time a head was severed, a new one arose, until there were twelve heads, each laughing wildly, each spewing fire and smoke. With every new head that arose, another child would step forward to do battle.

The village and forest were obscured in a thick haze of sulfurous fog, so that the villagers could no longer see their children as they fought against the Dragon. The monster's thick, dark blood covered the ground, making it hard for the champions to stand upright as they fought. Though their strength flagged, the children's spirits remained strong as they fought alongside one another.

When the twelfth head was severed, the Dragon uttered an earth-shaking groan, and his huge body shuddered. No more heads sprouted. A huge crevice opened in the earth, swallowing his bleeding body. Yet from the earth's depths, sounding through the black blood and the brown fog, there came his cry,

"I will return!"

Exhausted and covered with burns and wounds, the children clung to one another, too tired to jubilate. The village was hidden in a wreath of darkness and smoke, so they made their way to the cave in which their smithy was hidden. With only their shields for pillows, they lay down and fell into a deep sleep.

For months, the villagers searched for the twelve boys and girls who had so valiantly slain the Dragon, but to no avail. No one but the twelve children knew of the cave in which they slept. So after a long and fruitless search, their parents believed that the young champions had been swallowed up by the earth, like the body of the Dragon.

Many years passed. No longer harassed by the Dragon, the villagers plowed new fields, and grazed young lambs and placid cows in the flower-filled meadows. The memory of the Dragon grew faint as the village grew more prosperous and became a town. Grandmothers might still tell tales of the monster on chill winter nights, but few believed that he had ever existed. People avoided the brackish swamp where his lair had once been, but no one remembered why.

One day a traveler from a distant land lost his way in the forest. It grew dark, so he decided to spend the night in the woods near the swamp, and find his path by daylight. He gathered dry twigs and fallen branches and struck his flint and steel to start a fire. As the fire grew, a spark leaped out of the ring of stones the man had formed and began to glow several paces away.

The traveler ran to the new fire so as to put it out, but he noticed that the spark had ignited a thick, dark liquid that bubbled out of the earth. He watched it for some time, and saw that it burned with a warm and steady glow. A drinking cup's worth of this thick, oily substance sustained a fire that lasted much longer than two armfuls of wood.

In the morning, he filled his wineskin with the strange fluid and found his way to what once had been the village, and was now a thriving little city. He called upon the mayor and the city fathers, who gathered around him as he poured the contents of his wineskin into a metal bowl and lit a fire that lasted for a day and a night. Though some objected to the thick brown haze that settled over the town square as the fire burned, all agreed that a wonder had been discovered. No one could explain why the swamp had never been explored up until now.

Word spread quickly. The path to the swamp was trodden by thousands of feet as people came to gather up the fuel that bubbled so bountifully out of the earth, like water from a spring. The mayor ordered that a wall be built around the swamp, and that each who entered should pay a fee for the munificent oil.

Before long, it was discovered that the dark liquid bubbled up in other swamps as well. In those places in which it did not issue forth of itself, men found ways of drilling deeply into the earth, drawing it out as they once had drawn water from under the ground. Then it was determined that the deserts held more oil under their sand than all of the swamps combined. Wherever there were wastelands, there was oil to be found.

Men became ever more clever in their methods of forcing the fluid out of the earth. The more they drew out, the more they needed. The discovery of such a plentiful and long-lasting fuel led people to contrive new uses for it. While workers had once been content to labor by hand at a slow and steady pace, now it happened that factories were built, and many people had to work rapidly to keep up with rushing machines powered by the remarkable fuel. Boats plowed through the seas, carriages moved as though by themselves over the land, and huge vessels with smooth metal bodies soared in the skies, all devouring the black oil as quickly as it was forced out of the earth's depths.

A dull brown haze settled over the cities where the oil was consumed, and gradually spread, wraith-like, over the whole world. The sun's light was dimmed, but people were now so preoccupied and busy that they rarely looked up at the sooty and somber sky.

The most remote parts of the world were explored, and many a wild place was crisscrossed by roads conveying those who searched for oil. Even lands long covered by the sea were drilled until they yielded their dark treasure. Boats as large as cities were filled with oil, and cumbersomely bore their black burden over stormy seas.

It happened that, as one of these clumsy boats wended its way through turbulent waters, it ran aground on sharp rocks. Its thick skin was punctured, and its cargo of thick oil began to ooze out like black blood from a wound.

The wild waves carried the oil far and wide across the storm-filled waters.

Like a serpent, the ooze slithered through the sea, winding itself around all that it touched. Creatures smaller than the eye could see were smothered by the black mire. The fish who swallowed them in turn choked on the oil, and helplessly floated up to the ocean's surface. Seals who ate the fish were covered by the dark fluid, and could no longer swim. Birds who swooped down upon the seals had their feathers soaked by the thick oil, and could no longer fly.

The waves that crashed against the shore cast the oil upon the beaches, where it spattered over flowers and trees, extinguishing their life. Wherever the dark ooze spread, there was death and desolation. And bubbling out of the ever-spreading slick of the Dragon's blood some could hear, in a raspy whisper, the words,

"I will return!"

Though they were whispered, the words were heard in a cave far from the darkening ocean, where twelve children had been sleeping for a thousand years. They awakened, and with hardly a word, they set about their task. Preparing themselves for the coming battle, they left the cave, and began their long march to the sea.

As they marched, a silent and determined group, other young people watched, and the bolder among them joined the assemblage.

By the time they reached the ocean, they were a hundred thousand strong. They were ready, once again, to contend with the Dragon.

But this time, instead of swords, they held scrub brushes in their right hands. And this time, instead of shields, they held buckets of soapy water in their left hands. Instead of armor, they were clothed from head to foot in waterproof suits.

Some groups began to wade into the sea, to rescue the helpless creatures covered in the Dragon's blood. Other groups went out in boats to skim the Dragon's blood off the watery surface, so that light and air might return to the ocean depths. And still other groups scrubbed the birds, the seals, the fish, the rocks and sand, dissolving the Dragon's blood and making the sea and earth fresh and clean again.

One day, children, you, too, may join those champions as they battle once again with a new Dragon. For unless they have died, they are cleaning still today.

The End

Other books of Eugene Schwartz published by Rudolf Steiner College Press:

Adolescence: The Search for the Self and Weaving the Social Fabric of the Class
Seeing, Hearing, Learning: The Interplay of Eye and Ear in Waldorf Education
Rhythms and Turning Points in the Life of the Child
The Waldorf Teacher's Survival Guide
What You Didn't Learn in Teacher Training
Plays for Children and Communities
Wish, Wonder and Surprise

Book orders may be made through Rudolf Steiner College Bookstore:
Tel: 916-961-8729, Fax: 916-961-3032
Online orders: www.steinercollege.edu

More from Eugene Schwartz:
Information on Eugene's talks and story-telling workshops, articles, videos, and podcasts can be found at his web site www.millennialchild.com.

More from Kris Carlson:
Individual commissions for original paintings, murals and all other inquiries may be discussed with Kris at kris4769@gmail.com.

Rudolf Steiner College Press (RSCP) is the publishing house of **Rudolf Steiner College**, one of America's leading Waldorf teacher education colleges. It is also a center for anthroposophical studies and transformative adult education.

Located on a beautiful thirteen acre campus in Fair Oaks, California, just outside of Sacramento, the College offers students a wide range of full-time and part-time educational opportunities including Waldorf teacher training, personal enrichment classes, workshops and cultural events. The campus includes a bookstore, the press, bio-dynamic garden and orchard, a performance hall, a student housing complex, and a LifeWays Children's Center.